Makeup

THIS IS A CARLTON BOOK

Published in 2015 by Carlton Books Limited
20 Mortimer Street
London W1T 3JW

10 9 8 7 6 5 4 3 2 1

A CIP catalogue record for this book is available from the British Library.

ISBN 978 1 78097 509 2

Text by Caroline Jones
Senior Executive Editor: Lisa Dyer
Managing Art Director: Lucy Coley
Picture Researcher: Emma Copestake
Production Controller: Janette Burgin
Designer: Emma Wicks
Cover Design: Lisa Layton

Printed in Dubai

You **Tutorial**

Makeup

▶ Your guide to the best instructional YouTube videos

**CARLTON
BOOKS**

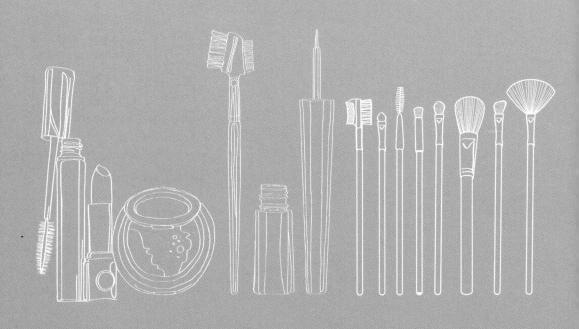

Contents

Introduction   6

Skin and Base   8

Whole Face   21

The Eyes Have It   59

Lips and Cheeks   81

Nail It   90

Tools of the Trade   97

Get The Look   109

Credits   128

INTRODUCTION

How to use this book

These days there's a YouTube video tutorial for everything. Especially when it comes to beauty. Indeed, if YouTube didn't exist, it's likely makeup addicts would have to invent it. In the space of just a few years, the webcam-friendly video sharing site has soared in popularity and proved the perfect medium for makeup tutorials, detailing step-by-step guides to help viewers master tricky beauty techniques.

But with such a vast array of makeup vlogs out there – all promising to teach you professional-style product application skills from the comfort of your home – it can be more than a little confusing to work out which are the best ones to watch.

So if you're unsure who is the best makeup artist or beauty guru when it comes to amazing insider tips and tricks, *YouTutorial* is here to help.

This handy book carefully selects more than 100 of the best makeup videos ever uploaded to YouTube, so you can find and watch them fast – without wasting countless hours trawling the internet.

Want to learn the best vlog to teach you the perfect "cat eye" flick with eyeliner or to create a perfectly contoured celebrity-style foundation base? Need a foolproof lesson in fixing false lashes, or covering up under-eye bags once and for all? We've got the perfect video for you, right here.

The tutorials in this book are curated from the most successful beauty vloggers on the web, with many videos selected because they boast the highest number of viewer hits. Plus, you'll also find hidden gems from some of the less well known, up-and-coming vloggers, who have stand-out techniques and are well on their way to cult beauty guru status. All of which means you will find plenty of great new YouTube channels to subscribe to.

Each video review explains why the clip is a must-see, along with relevant details of the vlogger behind it, and has both a URL address and QR code so you can instantly find and view the real thing.

So, what are you waiting for – discover, log on and get glam!

How to View the Clips

Each entry is accompanied by a QR code, which you can scan with your digital device using apps such as Quick Scan, QR Reader or ScanLife. Alternatively there is a short URL address which you can type into your browser. Unfortunately the adverts preceding some of the clips are unavoidable but it's usually possible to skip them after a few seconds.

SKIN AND BASE

Skincare, Foundation
and Contouring Tutorials

Contour and Highlight like Kim Kardashian

Vlogger Wayne Goss teaches
a masterclass on contouring

Makeup artist extraordinaire Wayne Goss teaches
you how to create Kim's signature look – glowing
skin, bright eyes and chiselled cheekbones – with
a masterclass on highlighting and contouring.
Kim always seems to boast the angelic "glow from
within" look that, in large part, has to do with her
highlighter application to emphasize the high points
of the face. Although Wayne's delivery style is
friendly and straight from the hip, this video is a little
scary for first-timers as it involves so much light
concealer and dark contour. However, the approach
absolutely works – the key is to apply it in thin layers
and blend, blend, blend, so the whole face looks
naturally structured.

Acne Foundation Routine for Flawless Skin

Cassandra Bankson's ultimate guide
for covering spots

Cassandra Bankson became a YouTube star when her amazing video on how she covered up her own severe acne with foundation went viral. Now the model and student has a comprehensive archive of videos on her channel DiamondsAndHeels14. In this full coverage tutorial Cassandra bravely bears her very spotty, inflamed, red skin for all to see, and then explains her foolproof way to hide it, including the best primer to make sure the make up stays put, the right coverage foundation and her fingertip application technique, mixing colours, applying concealer to any remaining red spots and setting everything using two different shades of loose powder.

http://youtu.be/ex33wtqnNz8

Simple Routine for Perfect Skin

Achieve picture perfect skin
with A Model Recommends

Photo-flawless skin is a model's livelihood, so who better to talk you through the ultimate morning and evening skincare routine than model Ruth Crilly. In this episode of her A Model Recommends vlog, Ruth reveals the regime she's stuck to throughout her 12-year modelling career. Rather than talking in the confusing jargon of skincare adverts, Ruth strips the information down to the basics, as she discusses her three failsafe steps to perfect skin for any skin type: Cleansing balm, serum and moisturizer. Many of the products she recommends are from luxury brands, but pleasingly there are also a few high street heroes in there too.

Heavy Glam Highlight – Contour like a Pro

Kasey Palmer shows the easy way
to contour

Straight-talking Arizonan mum-of-four Kasey Palmer's makeup tutorials are short, sassy and show you up-close shots of the area she's working on so you don't miss a thing. She even has her own line of cosmetics, StillGlamorus. This is the video tutorial to watch if you find the contouring method difficult to follow as it demonstrates her own much simpler, section-by-section method that's ideal for beginners. She shows how to highlight and then shade for a natural but still very glam look. There are moments in the middle where you can't believe the makeup will all come together in one look, but with her mantra of "blend, blend, blend" Kasey nails it and the result is a gorgeously contoured face.

http://youtu.be/iaCj1kYkptc

Conceal Dark Circles on Any Skin Tone

Tiffany D's masterclass on banishing eye bags

Tiffany of MakeupByTiffanyD is a self-taught makeup artist and beauty product junkie from Atlanta, with a super-accessible delivery style that makes accomplished makeup application seem easy. This tutorial is a lifesaver for anyone who's ever cursed their undereye circles. Her 12-minute vlog breaks down how-to-use colour-corrector shades – such as green, lilac, yellow and orange – to maximum effect when it comes to concealing. She then shows how to mask even the worst dark circles and camouflage areas of puffiness, and has her say on whether it really matters if you apply concealer before or after foundation.

How to Bronze Your Face

Pixiwoo's recipe for a healthy summer glow

Samantha and Nic Chapman are the makeup artist sisters behind one of the best-known YouTube beauty channels – Pixiwoo. Their back-to-basics videos are a must-watch for any beauty beginner. In this quick and easy guide to getting a sun-kissed look, we're shown how even pale skin can look tanned – without going orange. You start by using a tinted moisturizer, which because it's sheer can be a couple of shades darker than your natural skin colour. And when picking a bronzer shade, Sam advises thinking about the colour you go when you tan in the sun, and choosing matte rather than shimmery products. We even learn how to apply a smattering of fake freckles!

http://youtu.be/dk9KWFdykEU

Make Pores Disappear in Seconds

Get airbrushed, perfect skin
with Wayne Goss

Makeup artist Wayne Goss discovered many of his beauty secrets after struggling with acne in his twenties. Long before he became famous for his amazing contouring transformations, he spent many hours creating foolproof techniques to conceal blemishes. Here Wayne explains that makeup won't block pores, because it simply sits on the skin rather than sinks into it. He then demonstrates how applying foundation normally makes pores look more obvious, but by using a soft brush and a buffing, circling motion – in both directions – they seem to disappear. Watch this video and you'll be able achieve that poreless, flawless look that you see in magazines – no airbrushing required!

http://youtu.be/EmZm3vwrF8Q

Skincare Routine for Clear, Glowing Skin

The secrets of Fleur DeForce's radiant complexion

Good-looking makeup starts with great skin and vlogger Fleur DeForce reveals she has what's known in the beauty industry as "normal" skin – which means that although it's not overly dry or oily, she does still suffer from the occasional breakout, flaky area or oily patch. So to keep her skin looking in tip-top condition, the Brit beauty guru has come to highly value an effective skincare routine. In this video discover Fleur's pick of scrubs, spot treatments, moisturizers, eye creams, oils and face masks. You won't want to miss finding out about her obsession for using a cleansing balm, which takes less time than using a face wipe, and is actually good for your skin as it helps soften it.

http://youtu.be/4JYyl5vQfGl

Colour-Correcting Tutorial

Learn the art of clever concealment with Julia Graf

Ever spotted a mint-coloured concealer at the beauty counter and wondered how to apply it without looking a little green around the gills? Well, Julia Graf of beauty and lifestyle vlog MissChievous is here to share her insider knowledge on colour theory. She explains why using different shades to hide a variety of blemishes and imperfections will give you a more flawless finish than just using one shade that matches your skin tone. The Swiss-Canadian goes on to demonstrate how to create a seamless base, without a hint of dark circles or redness showing through your foundation. You'll also learn a clever trick for mixing your regular liquid foundation with a little liquid highlighter to give skin a luminescent finish.

Invisible Foundation Tutorial

Wayne Goss shares the
secret of flawless skin

Using makeup to create a smooth surface that actually looks like skin is a tricky skill to master, but with this masterclass from Wayne Goss, you can perfect the art of faking a flawless complexion, without the heavy caked-on makeup look that full coverage foundations and powders can give. The professional makeup artist explains how to hide areas of redness and broken capillaries with just one product, so that you can create an even skin tone using less than half the amount of foundation you normal use. This video on the Brit's gossmakeupartist channel is filmed in HD so you can see just how natural and perfect the finished look is.

http://youtu.be/QO3IRnleRIY

How to Control Oily Skin

Cassandra Bankson's techniques
for combating shine

It's not just teenagers who have oily skin, unfortunately many of us continue to battle against grease and spots throughout our adult lives. US model and vlogger Cassandra Bankson has spent years learning how to handle problem skin and she's happy to let you in on her discoveries. A major conundrum many people face is how to handle oil outbreaks when out-and-about without ruining their makeup – luckily Cassandra's found the one must-have product that makes dealing with grease on-the-go a breeze – blotting papers. She's also rounded up the best products and cleansing techniques to use at home, so that you're less likely to suffer from an oil breakout when you are wearing makeup.

http://youtu.be/enrmc4_hk3k

Your Best Base Ever

The pro way to perfect skin
with Kandee Johnson

Mum-of-four Kandee Johnson is a huge beauty star and impressively manages to combine multiple roles as a mother, makeup artist and vlogger. She believes that just as an artist has to make sure their canvas is primed before they paint on it, the same is true for makeup artists, so she created this ultimate guide to a perfect base, covering everything from primer to contouring in seven steps. Some steps may be daunting for makeup novices, but as Kandee says, "you don't need to do every step if you don't want to, you can pick and choose your makeup wearing level!"

http://youtu.be/t0nb0KqxnII

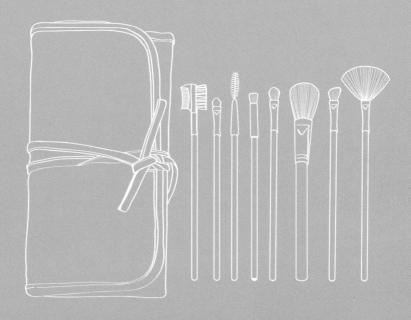

WHOLE FACE

Makeup Looks for Different Occasions

Get Approachable Glamour

Mally Roncal's lowdown on looking polished all day long

Celeb makeup artist Mally Roncal is one of the hottest makeup professionals in the beauty industry, with her own super-successful YouTube channel, Mally TV. She even has her own line of makeup, Mally Beauty, and has done so many fashion shows and beauty shoots for magazines, you can be sure her techniques and tips really work. Here she creates a simple, lasting look that can take you from a shopping trip to the red carpet. Includes great tips on how to brighten your face and get a soft smoky eye – and how to make blue eyes really pop using a navy blue eyeliner.

http://youtu.be/LleLfhyzkTE

Look Gorgeous for a Night Out

Pull out all the stops with
Tanya Burr's red-hot look

Tanya Burr has trained with professional makeup artists and worked for high-end beauty brands such as Laura Mercier and Clinique. Her bold eye makeup looks are top-notch. Here the bubbly Brit reveals her all-time favourite evening makeup look, one she promises will "make you feel really, really, gorgeous". She starts by creating the perfect "flawless" base, before showing how to shape defined "Cara Delevingne" style brows using powder and an angled brush. Highlights include how to use black eyeshadow next to the lid lashes instead of a gel eyeliner for a softer, more smouldering look, plus a clever technique involving drawing a black triangle in the corner of your eye for the ultimate glamorous eye definition. She finishes with blackcurrant lips. Simply stunning.

http://youtu.be/R6eNKA67-_8

Bridal Makeup Tutorial

Stun on your big day
with Sona Gasparian

If you're after makeup looks that are wearable, feminine and pretty, Sona Gasparian and her Youtube channel MakeupBySona is your girl. Here she provides a fabulous guide to getting a gorgeous look on your wedding day, explaining: "I think this is the perfect bridal look – something I would wear on myself". She then explains how brides can look polished in their photos but not over-made-up in the flesh, using blending and softening techniques for winged eyeliner and shadow. Interestingly she applies full eye-makeup before she uses foundation and concealer on the rest of the face, and employs a vitamin spray to soften the whole look, before highlighting and bronzing for a contoured finish.

http://youtu.be/PVhNlpPkzXM

Modern Retro Makeup

Marlena Stell's kooky take
on 1950s style

Self-styled "Makeup Geek" Marlena Stell is a former
school teacher, a background that shows in her
ultra-helpful videos on everything from beauty basics
to celebrity-inspired looks. Marlena descibes this
tutorial as the "perfect glamorous, vintage look that will
look good on everyone". After a simple base, she shows
how to get gorgeous 1950s-style pale pink eyes, with
cat-style eyeliner using a crafty bent eyeliner brush that
makes application so much easier. She also shares her
secrets for making your eyes look brighter using white
liner on the inner lids and red – yes, red – under the
lower lash line for a modern twist. She finishes with
bright red glossy lips and a funky 1950s headband.

"No Makeup" Makeup

Perfect barely-there
beauty with Bubz

Irish vlogger Lindy Tsang of Bubzbeauty has become a much-loved beauty star with her cute, easy-to-follow makeup tutorials. Here she shows how to create the no-makeup look, "because looking like a radiant natural beauty never goes out of style", she points out – adding that too much makeup can actually make you look older. After seeing her "pat-in" undereye circle cover technique and "press-in" foundation method, you'll never apply make up in the same way again. She also demos a clever way of holding the eyelid with a cotton bud instead of your fingers while you apply eyeliner, and finishes with a light cream blush on the apples of her cheeks and a little lip gloss. Simple but highly effective.

http://youtu.be/Kp02tRP2XaI

How to Do Pin-Up Girl Makeup

Kandee Johnson goes all-out
for glamour

LA-based lifestyle vlogger Kandee infuses her colourful makeup tutorials with heaps of personality and humour, making her very easy to watch. Here she helps you achieve the ultimate screen siren look using frosty eyeshadow shades and black eyeliner that starts thin at the top inner lid, then gets thicker and wings out past the outer corners, for real wide-eyed glamour. She then fills in dark, defined eyebrows using an angled brush and powder and shows how to use a mixture of pink blush and creamy highlighter on the cheeks for that dewy look celebs love so much. Gorgeous.

Favourite Autumn Makeup

Invisible beauty courtesy of Elle Fowler

Since 2008, Elle Fowler's makeup tutorials on her YouTube channel AllThatGlitters have enjoyed millions of views thanks to her approachable personality and easy-to-follow style. Here she demonstrates her signature "au naturel" look, adjusted for autumn. Highlights include using a white base on her eyelids to ensure her eyeshadow "pops" even more, and how to line the lips with a neutral shade and then apply sheer lipstick and gloss, for a "barely there" but pretty finish. Elle shows that a "nude" look still takes some time and skill to apply – but is certainly worth the extra effort as the end results are a naturally beautiful face.

http://youtu.be/p1FAadSPk5w

Everyday Makeup

 Blair Fowler reveals her nude-look makeup secrets

Elle Fowler turned her younger sister on to YouTube, and now Blair has become a beauty guru in her own right, with her own super-successful channel Juicystar07. Here the all-American teen reveals how she achieves her fresh and flexible everyday look, starting with her eye primer secrets for long-lasting smudge-proof shadow. Her chatty, informal style makes beauty less of a mystery, while her insistence that you don't need expensive tools to get a great finish means she's a terrific starting point for anyone relatively new to makeup. Watch out for her extra up-close beginner's demo on applying liquid eyeliner.

A Night to Remember

Annie Jaffrey rocks
red carpet glamour

Beauty guru and vegan Annie Jaffrey started YouTube channel Annie's Beauty Life in 2011 and quickly garnered over 1 million views. The popular New York-based vlogger shares her makeup tricks through tutorials that are easy to follow and full of personality. Here she focuses on using shimmery eye colours to gradually build up a dramatic evening look. Her shadow technique is really simple and subtle – great for anyone who is afraid of experimenting with more than one eye colour at once. For a softer, smokier finish she applies shadow instead of pencil under the lids. Annie also reveals how to apply bronzer and blusher to give your face more definition in photographs, ending with statement shocking pink lips.

http://youtu.be/-bl4QnXxKrl

SOS Morning-After Look

Banish tiredness
with RachhLoves

Rachel of RachhLoves is a bubbly Toronto-based beauty vlogger and mum, who loves all things girly and glam and is a total makeup pro. This lifesaver look is perfect for the morning after the night before – and the best part is it takes just 10 minutes to apply, so you can enjoy a longer lie-in. Rachel breaks it down into simple steps, presented in captions, meaning you don't need to have the volume turned up – an added bonus on mornings when you're feeling a little delicate! Top tricks include using a light shimmery highlighter all over eyelids, a pale vanilla shadow along the brow line and a white kohl liner in the bottom waterline.

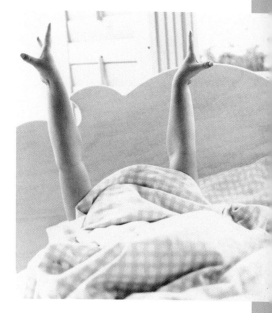

http://youtu.be/hQVwCBiRjSI

Get a Natural Glow

Zoella demos her tricks for looking naturally lovely

Adorably elfin Brit Zoe Sugg has a bubbly personality and great sense of humour, which has made her YouTube channel Zoella a huge success. The fact her makeup techniques are spot-on also helps! Zoe's not a professional makeup artist but her enthusiasm and self-taught skills means she's a great go-to for younger girls experimenting with makeup techniques for the first time. This fresh-faced look uses foundation, concealer, bronzer and blusher, and she shows how to blend down your neck for a natural look. We also learn to tidy eyebrows in seconds, using a felt-tip-style brow pen and how to get a glossy look with eyeshadow crayons and lip gloss. Simple but gorgeous.

http://youtu.be/CrOAVLICvhw

Gold and Silver Sparkle

LetzMakeup's statement
Christmas party look

Want to stand out at the office party? You're in safe hands with professional makeup artist Siobhán McDonnell, aka LetzMakeup, who has fast become one of YouTube's most successful beauty vloggers. Her popular videos are jam-packed with professional tips but are also very daring and directional. This party look has silver, gold, glitter, lashes, sparkle, gems... the lot! But the results are not OTT, as Siobhán says: "it looks really class". Indeed, this look isn't just for Christmas – the effect is sensational rather than seasonal so you could easily wear it to any party. Watch out for Siobhán's great brush technique advice for perfect eyeliner, and tips for coating both sides of fair eyelashes with mascara.

Wedding Makeup Look for Darker Skin

How BritPopPrincess became
a blushing bride

Wedding makeup is tricky – you need a look that will last through any emotional moments and take you from day to night without appearing too caked on. For her own wedding, hugely successful British vlogger Patricia Bright called in fellow vlogger The Queen Hadassah, aka Esther, to do her bridal makeup. And in this tutorial, filmed one year after the wedding, the expert pair team up once more to offer tips for those, like Patricia, with darker skin tones who want to glow on their big day. Top insights include contouring for darker skins and how to achieve peachy glossy lips.

http://youtu.be/YxWOhvFwuzU

Day to Night in 6 Steps

Lily Pebbles' effortless evening transformation tips

When British student Lily Pebbles began her YouTube beauty channel she had no idea it would soon go from hobby to full-time job, involve her in collaborations with brands such as ASOS and win her a Best Independent Beauty Blogger award. Here she shows how using just a touch of concealer, some pressed powder and blusher can create a great base for any look. She then adds a creamy eye crayon all over the lids, blended with a brush, and under the lash line as a liner, plus adds a bit of volume to her hair using some dry shampoo. To finish, a combo of neutral lipstick and gloss add polish and lip volume, helping you seamlessly slip from work into playtime.

Vintage Glam Makeup

Girl-next-door to glamourpuss
with Lauren Luke

YouTube sensation Lauren Luke gets some 77 million viewers on her channel panacea81, where she demonstrates all her favourite makeup looks in her down-to-earth Northern style – she even has her own makeup range now. Here she segways between inspiring application tips, such as steadying your hand with your little finger on your face while applying eyeliner, and musing on the "beautiful" smells reaching her from the kebab shop on the street below! The end result is still perfectly professional with vampy retro eyes, using a pale, shimmery shadow, winged eyeliner and black mascara, plus neutral but glossy lips.

http://youtu.be/dvodbogykWc

Bridal Makeup for Less

 Emily Noel Eddington shows how affordable makeup can look A-list

Emily started her career as a US news anchor before leaving to run her hugely successful YouTube beauty channel, emilynoel83, full-time. Advocating the belief that "the confidence makeup brings can be life-changing", her inspiring vlogs often include suggestions for consumers wanting to save some cash. Here she creates a classic bridal romantic look using products you can buy cheaply from pharmacies on one half of her face, and pricier ones on the other half. By the time she has finished, you can't tell the difference between her expensive eyes, cheeks or lips, and those on the budget half – proving you don't have to spend a fortune to look a million dollars on your wedding day.

http://youtu.be/zSb9DPAejN4

Fresh and Simple

MissGlamorazzi plays it low key
with this natural look

Vlogging since 2009, Ingrid Nilsen has become a go-to expert when it comes to quick and easy beauty tips. Her channel MissGlamorazzi is packed with helpful tutorials on everything from organizing your makeup to how to make a summer hair mask out of mangoes. And if you're still struggling to perfect your no-fail everyday face, "girl-next-door gorgeous" Ingrid is here to help. This instructional video takes you swiftly through all of the necessary steps for looking fresh-faced and beautiful in a flash – including a secret line of black eyeliner on your upperlid waterline to make your lashes look naturally fuller.

http://youtu.be/nDuYTNPSNdg

Dramatic Clubbing Makeup

Jessica Harlow's eye-catching party look

Perhaps it's the fact that Jessica Harlow's tone is always perky or that you feel like you're getting advice from your older sister when you listen to her – either way her popular beauty videos are easy to follow and will leave you looking ultra-glamorous. Here she demos a special night out triple-winged eyeliner effect, using shadow to map out the shape before applying black liquid liner and then adding some shimmery brown and lilac eyeshadow. She finishes with white liquid liner and false lashes for extra drama. The result is a gorgeously daring look that's sure to get you noticed in the crowd.

http://youtu.be/i3lnxsv0kKA

Heat-Friendly Makeup Tutorial

Kasey Palmer's summer look
with staying power

In this video StillGlamorus's Kasey Palmer gives you the lowdown on how to adjust your makeup for days when the temperature really spikes. If you're blessed with blemish-free skin she in fact advises you to go au naturel – apart from SPF – but for those of us with less-than-perfect complexions she recommends a BB cream, a wonder Blemish Base which promises to do the job of five or six beauty staples: moisturizer, primer, sunscreen, skin treatment, concealer and foundation! Then cover any spots showing though using a little more product and a blending brush. Kasey also shows how to lightly apply bronzer, blusher, brow pencil, waterproof mascara and a touch of sheer lip balm for a look that lasts even when the sun blazes.

http://youtu.be/THkdeWpoGbg

Office-Appropriate Makeup

Chloe Morello demos her smart work-wear look

Chloe Morello is a hugely popular 20-something Australian who first got into makeup at the tender age of 4. Her laid-back but breezy and beautiful-to-watch tutorials have meant that in just two years she's become one of Down Under's most successful YouTube vloggers. In this clip she creates a great look for the office, perfect for when you want to look groomed and professional, with just a hint of glamour. Chloe's a fan of mineral makeup, because it gives great coverage and colour but is good for your skin at the same time. Watch out for her amazing dot eyeliner application technique, which creates the illusion of a thicker lash line and makes eyes look incredible, and also the funky fan-shaped blusher brush she uses for naturally flushed cheeks.

Summer Day to Night

Weylie's guide to a practical
look that lasts

Vlogger Weylie is the perfect mix of zany and practical which means she's big on helpful step-by-steps but doesn't shy away from trying new things. In this useful video she starts with primer to ensure her makeup stays put long into the night and follows with foundation, applied with a brush, then concealer under the eyes and a oil-controlling pressed powder applied with a large brush to set everything. Weylie then goes all out with her eyes, using shadow, liner, falsies and mascara – including a turquoise pop of colour under the lash line. A neutral tea rose shade of lips finishes this fresh summer day-into-evening look that you'll want to try.

http://youtu.be/zZJr4Y9GNxl

Evening Makeup Routine

Look amazing on a night out
with Anna Gardner

Brit Anna Gardner, founder of the hit YouTube vlog
ViviannaDoesMakeup, is a girl after your own heart –
obsessed with makeup and downright crazy about
skincare. Here she shares her Saturday night look,
including a great starter tip about avoiding any
moisturizer or foundation which contains SPF,
because they can show up very white in artificial
lighting, especially if people are taking photos. She
plumps for powders over gels and creams for better
nighttime staying power on eyes and cheeks, but
doesn't set her matte finish foundation with powder
to keep the base soft and dewy. Bronzer is applied
liberally – with Anna's top tip of taking it with you in
your handbag for toilet touch-ups.

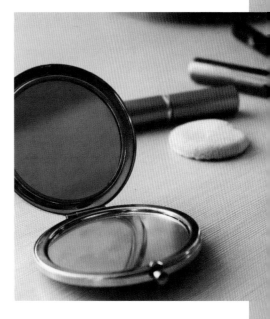

Easter Makeup Idea

Go girly for spring
with Bethany Mota

Bethany Mota is the quintessential girl next door. She has a fun, kooky style, and her channel is packed full of helpful how-tos that are a particularly valuable resource if you're a younger viewer hoping to figure out the basics. For this video she demos her favourite Spring/Easter makeup look, plumping mainly for high street brands such as Cover Girl and Maybelline, to make it an affordable and achievable look for anyone. After a simple skin base, Bethany uses pale peaches and pinks on her eyes with a little winged eyeliner, a dab of fresh pink cheek cream and finally a touch of babydoll pink lipgloss. Simple and sweet.

http://youtu.be/aqC-zrS5mAE

Beach Party Makeup

 Ingrid Nilsen's peachy summer evening look

Here, MissGlamorazzi's Ingrid Nilsen outlines her beach party look with her trademark infectious enthusiasm. She begins using a spring water facial spritz – perfect to cool, hydrate and soothe the skin after a day in the sun. Then she uses a pore and oil reducing primer to perfect her skin texture in the heat, a light-reflecting concealer to hide dark circles and an eye primer to stop eye makeup sliding off, setting everything with a powder foundation. Instead of lots of eye colours, she sticks to one neutral shimmery gold shadow, a little brown eyeliner on the upper waterline only, then waterproof mascara, adding a touch of bronzer and blush. This holiday look is then finished with a sheer coral lippie.

http://youtu.be/k9wl8RpnhK0

Natural Back-to-School Makeup

Lo Bosworth's groomed and gorgeous student look

Lo Bosworth's cheery style has lots of appeal for younger viewers, who will love this simple student makeup tutorial. For a totally natural look Lo only uses primer – no foundation. Instead she applies a light covering of concealer, just on the parts of the face it's needed, applying it with a brush sprayed with a little toner and using a buffing action to create a photoshop finish on skin. A few strategic lines of cream bronzer help to contour the face, and Lo then layers two blushers, a cream followed by a powder, for a healthy pink glow. A slick of the same cream bronzer for eyelids with waterproof mascara is all she uses for the eyes, while lips are simply stained with a little cream blush and shiny balm.

http://youtu.be/cRZguV3b1hk

New Year's Eve Makeup

Party on with
Lily Pebbles

"New Year's Eve is all about the glitter and the shimmer," exclaims vlogger Lily Pebbles, and this look is fabulously festive without being OTT, with rich plum and taupe tones that really make the eyes pop. Lily is known for her honesty – she won't promote any old products on her vlog unless she really uses them herself – and here she demos the full look she herself has worn on New Year's Eve. Even better she covers everything from hair and makeup to sequined nails and fragrance. Don't miss her top tip for ensuring makeup lasts all night and how to ensure you pick a foundation that will work in the bright nighttime lights.

http://youtu.be/YpJiREQJ-oE

Festival Makeup

Natural rock chic style
with Louise Redknapp

Former singer Louise Redknapp and makeup artist Kim Jacob created their Wild About Beauty makeup range with an aim to "celebrate natural looking beauty", which makes them the perfect advisors for those wanting to create a simple and summery festival look that channels inner glow. Here Louise plays the part of model, while Kim explains and demonstrates how to use the precious few products stashed in your bag to maximum effect to create a look that will last and protect your skin from the sun, even when you're exposed to the elements. Top tips include using a super-hydrating tinted moisturizer with SPF of at least 20 and a cream blusher for lips and cheeks.

http://youtu.be/owbvqr6RSp4

Bobbi Brown Full-Face Makeup Application

10 steps to perfection with Bobbi

If anyone knows about makeup, Bobbi Brown does, and this comprehensive tutorial explains how to look and feel your best in 10 simple steps that take you all the way from cleansing to blush, eyeliner and lips. "To me makeup is simple and amazing," explains the creator of the popular cosmetic brand. "I believe that all women are pretty without makeup and with the right makeup can be pretty powerful." Learn the founder's million-dollar secret to choosing the right moisturizer and foundation for your skin type, why she believes concealer is the "secret of the universe" and the best way to cover a blemish. Bobbi also offers top application tips, including always lining lips after lipstick for better definition and her three-colour rule for perfect eyeshadow – dark, medium and light.

http://youtu.be/V_iAG4BFyKc

Sick Days Hair and Makeup

Sneezy but stylish with
Bethany Mota

Feeling a bit under the weather? "Dr" Beth is here is ensure you don't look it. The popular vlogger has created a look that's super-easy to master and takes just a couple of minutes to apply, so it's simply perfect for days when you're a bit off-colour – or just feeling plain lazy! In what is probably the only makeup tutorial that includes chicken noodle soup and tea, Beth talks you through the entire look, from moisturizer and makeup to hair and comfy chic clothes. Useful tips include how to hide a red nose and eyes with concealer, preventing your skin from drying out and brightening pallid complexions.

http://youtu.be/0Tl79OunN18

Daytime Party Makeup

Sona Gasparian's
wearable glamour

Garden parties, weddings and barbecues throw up a beauty conundrum: how do you create party glamour without looking OTT? Smoky eyes, red lips and glitter are too heavy for these largely daytime occasions. So how do you get the balance right between fresh-faced and knock-'em-dead glitz? Thankfully beauty vlogger Sona Gasparian has got it all worked out. She's nailed the daytime fresh party face and with this easy-to-follow tutorial she explains how you can too. It's also a fun look with lots of individual lashes, super-glowy sheer skin coverage and pretty soft pink lips. And don't miss Sona's contouring tip for giving your jawline a slim-line shape.

Sparkly Glamour

Shine like a star with GlamLifeGuru Tati

A touch of genuine sparkle adds instant glamour to any look. Tati, the GlamLifeGuru, is known for her love of glitter and in this video she's here to unveil her top product picks and tips for a bit of glitz. You'll learn how to apply shimmer and shine to create a perfect look for a holiday, party or night on the town. Tati also demonstrates how to use your makeup brush as a guide for creating the perfect cat-eye shape and shares her top tip for ensuring your makeup stays in place all day long – skin primer and then a separate eye primer.

http://youtu.be/uipsoCqCFnc

1950s Makeup

Perfect vintage glamour
with Fleur DeForce

Old-school glamour never goes out of fashion. This Fifties' film star inspired look is one of beauty vlogger Fleur DeForce's favourites and she's got all the top techniques to perfect the style. The 1950s saw the rise of "the mask effect" in foundation and Fleur shares her top product pick for really good coverage. While the base was heavier, eye makeup was pared down, featuring dramatic feline liquid liner and natural-looking shadow. Inevitably, the focus of the look is a bright red pout and Fleur explains how to make your lips really pop, as well as how to tone down the overall look for more everyday glamour.

http://youtu.be/UbH7_vHBi1s

Birthday Makeup Tutorial

Be party perfect with
ViviannaDoesMakeup

It's your birthday – and Vivianna, aka Anna Gardner, has brought you a little gift in the form of a beauty tutorial that will help you create a look that ensures all eyes are on you when the party starts. The British blogger is usually a fan of quite minimalist makeup, but on her 24th birthday she wanted to go for something a little more sparkly and glam – including some full-on contouring because cheekbones were apparently on her birthday list! What makes Anna so watchable is that she's not afraid to say that she doesn't know it all – but all her tips are hard won through trial and error, so you know anything she recommends really works.

http://youtu.be/ZCw1i2VO2O0

Spring Makeup Tricks

Look fresh as a daisy
with Zoella

Lifestyle and beauty vlogger Zoe Elizabeth Sugg (aka Zoella) often gets asked: how did you get so gorgeous? And in this, the candid Brit assures us: "It's called makeup. I promise you underneath I look like Quasimodo." Even if the Brighton-based blogger is exaggerating, in this video Zoella fills us in on all those tips and tricks she uses for a daily transformation. Learn how to get a flawless complexion, add warmth with bronzer, apply eye makeup in seconds and use blusher to create a natural healthy glow. Typically, it's all delivered in Zoella's refreshingly honest manner – not many beauty "experts" would admit to having really dirty brushes!

http://youtu.be/5p2nqWZYBB0

Perfect Prom Makeup

 Jessica Harlow helps you become the belle of the ball

Vlogger Jessica Harlow likes to focus on timeless beauty, as opposed to throw-away trends. Here she creates a classic look that is perfect for an end-of-school party, as it looks fabulous up close and personal but also photographs brilliantly. But don't write this one off if you're a little more *ahem* mature than Sweet 16; this evergreen look is also great for cocktail parties. Highlights include hints about hiding blemishes, tips to stop eyeshadow creasing and how to make curls last for hours. Also, look out for Jessica's signature tap-and-blend application technique using just your "free beauty tools" – otherwise known as your fingers.

http://youtu.be/JL3T0lQRvc4

Big Event Makeup

Prep for perfection with Michelle Phan

There are some occasions in every woman's life when she wants to look her best. Whatever the event, be it a party, graduation or wedding, Michelle Phan has devised a 5-day plan to ensure you're looking stunning when the big day comes around. In order to ensure your skin, hair and body are perfectly prepared to party, Michelle has worked out a foolproof schedule. Highlights include how and when to: repair your skin using eye drops and an aspirin mask; brighten your complexion with a homemade lemon scrub; hydrate skin and hair; deal with the dreaded "peach fuzz"; and finally smooth and bronze your body.

http://youtu.be/xXU_yIBSpbw

Perkier Face Makeup

Lily Pebbles' ultimate
pick-me-up look

Vlogger Lily Pebbles is having a bad beauty day. She feels like her skin is bumpy and her dark circles are pronounced. But rather than spending the day avoiding other people, she's decided to take this opportunity to showcase the amazing transformative effect of one of her everyday makeup looks. The pick-me-up is perfect, from the best base for giving skin a healthy dewy look to applying heavier foundations so that they give a natural finish rather than a paint-like effect, through to finishing with a rich bronze-toned smoky eye to really warm up your look.

http://youtu.be/3JbLavEe26c

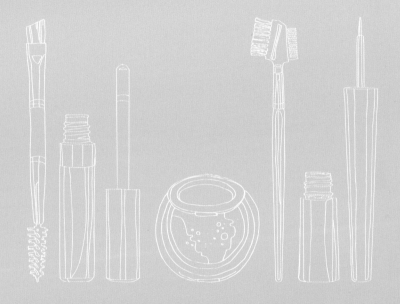

THE EYES HAVE IT

Eye Makeup Tutorials

Simple Eyeshadow Makeup Tutorial

Achieve eye-catching peepers
with Emma Pickles

British vlogger Emma Pickles' Euphoric Creations videos regularly get more than a million views. Not only is she a dead ringer for Katy Perry, her costume makeup tutorials are downright incredible. Here Emma pares it right down and demonstrates in just 2 minutes how to get perfect eyes. She explains how to build up eyeshadow colours from neutral to dark and then how to line eyes with matte black eyeshadow rather than liner, with a clever tip on combing through her mascara with a clean wand after applying to prevent unsightly clumping. Complex eye makeup can seem too tricky to attempt unless you're an expert, but Emma makes it look so easy, you'll wonder why you never tried before.

http://youtu.be/B8d9FYuZglQ

Eyeliner Variations – for All Eye Shapes

Become an eyeliner expert
with Julia Graf

Julia Graf is a genius with eye makeup, creating colourful looks on her MissChievous YouTube channel that aren't to be missed. In this video you get the ultimate eyeliner masterclass. From everyday and natural to more dramatic evening looks using liquid, gel, powder or pencils, Julia's got it all covered with her 12 key looks. Not only do you get a great guide on the classic winged eyeliner shape, she outlines the "double-wing" and the "Arab eye" – a kind of Cleopatra look in which the whole eye is circled. The "Sixties flick" is a must for getting the Twiggy look and the "colour pop" is a revelation – using a single line of bright coloured eyeliner next to black liner for a zing of colour without the need for additional eyeshadow. You'll be itching to experiment by the end.

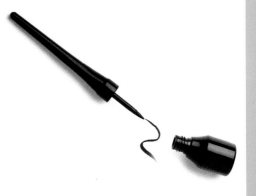

http://youtu.be/omhWDrYjKv0

Brighter, Larger-Looking Eyes

Look wide-eyed and wonderful
with Michelle Phan

Since Michelle Phan began posting tutorials in 2007, she's gained millions of followers for her videos. Her distinctive background music and special camera effects make her stand out from the crowd of online makeup artists. Here she shows how using a clever combination of white and black eyeliners can make eyes look instantly bigger and brighter – perfect if you want to avoid looking tired after an all-nighter. Her great tips include keeping your eyeliner lines thin, checking as you go that both eyes are even, and protecting your eyelid from transferred product when you apply mascara by using a bank card!

http://youtu.be/M4GVBkicnbU

How to Apply False Eyelashes

Leesha gives us the
lash lowdown

Quirky, punk-haired Leesha says she's drawn to bright and pretty things: "The brighter, the better!" she admits. On her highly successful YouTube channel, Xsparkage, she demos acid limes, dark cranberries, vivid pinks and electric blues – intimidating colours for many that she applies with ease. But if false eyelashes are the bane of your beauty regime, watch this in-depth 6-minute tutorial to learn how to quickly apply your falsies so that they look more natural and super-flattering. The simple step-by-step tips include how to cut lashes to fit your eye size and applying a line of eyeliner first to use as a sticking guide.

http://youtu.be/2_c0LI-gr64

How to Draw Perfect Arches

Julia Graf's foolproof tutorial
on awesome eyebrows

Fed up with your thin, sparse eyebrows? Watch makeup maven Julia Graf of MissChievous – whose natural brows are virtually nonexistent – construct a gorgeous, near-flawless symmetrical pair. She begins with a brow pencil in a shade lighter than her hair to outline the shape and then literally fills in the gaps – being careful not to go too dark to keep it natural. She then uses a sharp angled brush to blend and spread the product. Next comes a slightly darker shade of brow powder for definition at the bottom of the brow, which is blended and softened. The whole look is set and sealed with a clear mascara. Seriously impressive stuff.

http://youtu.be/tLTAKxv07B8

Shimmering Green Golden Eye Makeup

Master magnetic eye appeal
with Annie Jaffrey

Annie Jaffrey's YouTube channel is packed full of makeup tutorials that encourage viewers to think of their face as a blank canvas which can be transformed into whatever you like. This creative vlog meticulously details a soft shimmery green/gold eye look, which includes a masterclass on perfect shadow application and blending. "If you want to make it more intense and bold, darken up the shades you use on the eyelid crease and lower lash line," she advises. As well as the hot metal eyes, she also reveals her secret for using gold blusher and how to achieve perfect pink glossy lips.

http://youtu.be/GYh4Aqpey9U

The Perfect Eyeliner Flick

Work the winged-lid Twiggy look
with Siobhán McDonnell

Siobhán McDonnell, of LetzMakeup, is an incredibly talented makeup artist who specialized in painting at art college, which comes though in the creative and dramatic looks she favours. This amazing tutorial details two different ways to master the cat eye look, as well as how to ensure your wings are perfectly symmetrical. Irish beauty Siobhán draws her shape first with white eyeliner, so it's easy to correct mistakes, giving you a template for the right angle at which to apply your black liner. She also reveals how older women can rock this look, by using it to camouflage sags and creases.

http://youtu.be/QA4u5T1SouU

Matte Cranberry Eye Look

Tati's take on how red eyes can look surprisingly hot

Tati – of YouTube channel GlamLifeGuru – simply loves talking about all things beauty, from high-end products to low-end dupes – and everything in between. Here the *Allure* magazine expert advisor demos a red shadow look to suit all shades of eyes, explaining: "I've always stayed away from intense 'red toned' eye looks as I thought they were impossible to pull off, but due to the blending and matte finish, this look is surprisingly soft and pretty!" Tricks to watch out for include how she builds up colour using feather-light strokes, and pulls her temples up high with her fingers while she applies liquid eyeliner for greater precision.

Bronze and Orange Eyes with a Pop of Green

Rock rainbow eyes
with SimplYounique

Kerry vlogs frequently on highly successful YouTube channel, SimplYounique, covering a host of hair and makeup techniques. Her colours are often bold and bright, as this look shows, but her clever application makes them really work. Even if you think you can't wear wild shadow shades such as orange and green, after watching this expert tutorial, you'll think again. As well as always preparing your eyes with primer to make shadow last, Kerry is also a fan of multipurpose products and isn't afraid to use blusher for eyes and shadow for cheeks. Interestingly she also loves to keep lips nude to let the eyes speak for themselves.

http://youtu.be/mdopPyB3OCl

1970s-Inspired Eyes

Channel Abba with Lauren Luke's turquoise look

In her distinctive Geordie accent, vlogger Lauren Luke explains this funky retro look, complete with its bold blue-winged eye makeup. The result may not be for the faint-hearted, but it is perfect for a Seventies-themed party. Chatting casually in between her easy-to-follow makeup steps, bubbly Lauren talks about the weather, her weight loss and even where she's off to later that day! And her beauty tips are just as interesting as she expertly applies a bright turquoise shade of shadow on the top lid, teamed with vibrant orange under the eye. She also explains why beginners are better off using a cream or gel liner applied with a brush rather than a liquid pen.

http://youtu.be/32IZN5kWXmQ

Cat-Eye Makeup Tutorial

Instant eye appeal with
Charlotte Tilbury

Charlotte Tilbury is a renowned British makeup artist, often called on to paparazzi-proof clients such as Kristen Stewart and Victoria Beckham for the red carpet. The feline eye in this video is a look that Charlotte has made synonymous with the likes of Kate Moss. She explains: "The purpose is to elongate the eye, like a cat's. In doing so, you add intensity and the effect of an instant eye lift." To pull off the look she uses a smoky black eyeliner pencil – not liquid liner – applied with professional secrets including drawing small dots as a "wing" shape guide and using a cotton bud soaked in moisturizer to remove any mistakes.

https://youtu.be/fyIB5yXczWo

Pop of Colour: Periwinkle Blue

Become a blue-eyed
babe with Alli

Makeup-obsessed Alli shows viewers how to keep
their beauty regime fresh and fun. Her tutorials
on popular channel MakeUpByAlli are perfect for
those who love experimenting. Here she shows how
to apply sky-blue eye crayon all around the eyes to
create a striking and very pretty effect. She locks in
the colour by applying a little eyeshadow in the
same blue colour over the top of the crayon. Next
a shimmery bronze shadow is applied over the top
eyelid, before blending everything together, and
ending with a thin line of black liner on the top lid
next to the lash to help accentuate the vibrant
colour, plus lashings of jet-black mascara.

Dramatic Purple Smoky Eyes

Pull off perfect purple peepers with
MissChievous

Don't be a shrinking violet when it comes to this on-trend eyeshadow look. Julia Graf of MissChievous has an informal style of beauty vlogging that will quickly put you enough at ease to try this dramatic style. She outlines clever tips that will help you perfect this bold eye statement, such as using sticky tape to create a neat sharp edge and prevent colour bleeding. Overall this tutorial is easy to master even if you are a beauty novice, as Julia gently guides you through how to use different strokes to build up the layers of purple, lilac, white and dark blue, then finish with black and white kohl liner and mascara.

http://youtu.be/ff3X555hzaY

Easy Rainbow Eyes

Xsparkage demos how to surround your eyes with colour

The internet is bursting with rainbow eye makeup tutorials, but this one from the founder of Xsparkage is the proverbial pot of gold, as it is by far the easiest and the most effective in terms of eye-popping colour. It will come as no surprise that Leesha is a self-confessed makeup junkie, as her knowledge of shades and techniques is surely second to none. Watch mesmerized as she demonstrates how to use cream eyeshadow to keep highly pigmented mineral shadows in place and her technique for seamlessly blending the colours. Once completed, this attention-grabbing pink, yellow, green and blue look is guaranteed to wow.

http://youtu.be/mmwwgdzNvvo

Longer Eyelashes without Falsies

Cassandra Bankson's simple trick
for flutter-worthy lashes

Long, luscious lashes are the holy grail of beauty and while false lashes are great for an instant boost, they can be fiddly and time-consuming to apply. Luckily, blogger Cassandra Bankson has discovered one simple technique for your eyelashes that is so transformational people will presume they must be fake. In this eye-opening video Cassandra demonstrates how simply playing with colour and contrast, and learning to apply your eyeshadow in just the right way, can really amplify your lashes. It's so easy you'll wonder how you never knew about this trick before.

http://youtu.be/F6fRl-tTLNc

Everyday Makeup for Glasses Wearers

Get some specs appeal with
Tanya Burr

Those of us who wear glasses know that makeup looks different when behind the lenses of your frames. Thankfully vlogger Tanya Burr has perfected the art of choosing makeup that compliments glasses rather than fighting with the frames for attention. In this short masterclass Tanya talks us through a great everyday look for glasses-wearers and explains what you must do to avoid looking a bit – as Tanya puts it – "meh". Don't wear glasses? Well this tutorial is still a great subtle look that will take you from daytime to night, and Tanya's tips for perfecting a clean neat brow are simply too good to miss out on.

Blue Smoky Eye Makeup

Shake up your eye routine with Sona Gasparian

Are you stuck in a smoky eye rut? Step away from your palette of greys and blacks, and pick up some bright blue eyeshadow shades for a fresher, funkier take on the classic smoky look. Professional makeup artist Sona Gasparian guides you through her technique for cleverly blending different shades of blue and brown (her little secret for warming up an otherwise cool look), to create an eye effect that is dramatic enough for a night on the town, but less heavy than a classic smoky eye. You won't want to miss the native Californian's secret to glowy skin and her pick of the most fabulous fanned false lashes around.

http://youtu.be/LLnPln8_vMs

Bigger, Brighter Eyes

 Charlotte Tilbury's trick for faking
Bambi eyes

One of the questions makeup artist Charlotte Tilbury gets asked most frequently is: how can you cheat bigger, brighter eyes? This vlog has the answer to that million-dollar question. Learn how to create a wide-eyed Bambi look inspired by the evocative and alluring eyes of 1960s supermodel Veruschka and screen icons Elizabeth Taylor and Marlene Deitrich. Make your eyes miraculously appear bigger, brighter and more wide awake using simple tricks such as the best way to apply under-eye concealer with a dabbing motion, how to add depth with muted shades, and how to pick just the right nude-colour liner to work on your waterline.

http://youtu.be/0NKuH2oHJxo

Neutral Eye Makeup with a Pop of Blue

Be bold with Makeup Geek's summer look

Blue eyeshadow has gained something of a bad rep, ever since women in the 1980s stepped out with OTT blocks of blue shadow striped across their eyelids. But after watching this vlog from "makeup educator" Marlena, you'll never think of blue shadow in the same way again. Makeup Geek Marlena cleverly blends soft shimmery blues with neutral tan and taupe shades to create a look that's wearable from day to night and which will look great on everyone regardless of skin tone or eye colour. Just don't be tempted to pair this look with shoulder pads or you might go a retro step too far!

http://youtu.be/LZkYcpARez0

Futuristic Eyes

Don't follow fashion, create it… with LetzMakeup

Siobhán McDonnell of LetzMakeup wants to let you in on a little secret for creating show-stopping eyes in minutes, with this dramatic liner look. You would need an incredibly steady hand and a lot of patience to create this look using liquid liner, but Siobhán suggests trying some of the new eyeliner stickers in pretty designs that you can find in local pharmacies (drugstores) or online to make this futuristic look easy to achieve for even the most inexperienced makeup users. If Siobhán's liner design is a little over-the-top for your tastes, you should still check out this vlog as just the eyeshadow on its own would make for a more wearable but still "wow" party look.

http://youtu.be/qLJwFlJpuqA

Summer Eye Makeup Tutorial

Get pretty blue peepers
with Cassandra Bankson

Aspiring model Cassandra Bankson is fulfilling a quest to make everyone feel beautiful, with her highly detailed videos that always show the viewer exactly what she's using and how to apply it. Here she creates beguiling blue eyes, starting with primer and then pale blue shadow – which she explains brings out the colour in all shades of eyes – and then she reveals her method for dabbing darker shadow into the eye crease for a more precise application. Another great tip is applying white shadow around the tear duct to brighten the whole eye, making you look wide awake and well rested – even when you don't feel it!

http://youtu.be/S8omoDBcVUY

LIPS AND CHEEKS

Lipstick and Blusher Tutorials

How to Get Fuller Lips

Pixiwoo's recipe for
a plumper pout

Not only do Sam and Nic from Pixiwoo have a real knack for recreating celebrity makeup looks – with tutorials inspired by everyone from Angelina Jolie to Rihanna – they also know a thing or two about using makeup to cleverly enhance your natural features. Here Sam explains how to make lips look bigger, by using a primer base on them and then a neutral shade of liner, followed by a second slightly darker liner just outside the natural lip line. Then a neutral shade of lipstick is applied all over and a layer of pale gloss on top – resulting in lips that look miraculously fuller than nature intended.

http://youtu.be/xEUoMIb2Ixk

The Perfect Red Lip Tutorial

Get a stunning scarlet pout
with RachhLoves

Rachel of RachhLoves is a whizz when it comes to easy-to-follow but effective makeup tutorials and she is also full of really helpful "big sister" advice about boosting your body confidence. Red lips dial up the wow factor for any look, and this video provides a visual step-by-step on exfoliating lips with an old toothbrush, lining with lip pencil and then painting on the perfect punchy candy-apple-red pout. All the products she uses here are cheap pharmacy (drugstore) buys, and she ends with a handy tissue blotting trick for ensuring your lips boast better staying power.

From Cracked to Kissable Lips

Patricia Bright's prescription
for a super-soft pout

Patricia Bright's YouTube channel BritPopPrincess attracts so many views because she isn't afraid to share her own flaws along with the best fixes for them. Here she confesses that she often suffers from cracked, dry winter lips, revealing how the problem can be caused by air-con and central heating, as well as recommending the best products to soften and smooth them. Her top tip is to exfoliate your lips at night to remove the flakes, and then apply a thick layer of petroleum jelly to sink in overnight. She also suggests choosing glossy lipsticks over matte finishes to help condition lips during the day.

http://youtu.be/uJGLTb_cA78

Pinker Lips: 10 Different Ways

Enhance your natural pout
with AndreasChoice

Beauty isn't only about makeup. Here vlogger Andrea Brooks explains how to make your lips look naturally soft and rosy pink – a sign, she says, of youthfulness, good health and proper hydration. But don't be upset if your lips are a little on the pale side without makeup – Andrea's full of advice on how to restore, enhance and protect your natural lip colour, using everyday items from your kitchen and bathroom. Her natural beauty advice is practical but never preachy, and she also has a few cheats for getting a natural look with just a hint of makeup. Highlights include her virgin olive oil and sugar lip scrub home recipe and why you should always use lip balm or lipstick with a built-in SPF.

http://youtu.be/8feMUuMbd6E

Red Velvet Lips

 The art of lipstick-free red lips
with Kandee Johnson

This must-see vlog is the ultimate guide to creating smooth, rich red lips and it doesn't even involve any lipstick! Kandee Johnson named the look "Red Velvet Lips" because "the results are as delicious-looking as red velvet cake". All you need to achieve the vibrant colour is two lip liners – a cool red and a chocolate brown for depth – plus some blusher. Highlights of the tutorial include how to create a pin-up shape pout, choosing just the right shades to make your teeth look sparkling white, tips for preventing unsightly smearing and why you should always pat on some blusher to ensure the colour stays in place all day long.

http://youtu.be/yr-gDp2hx54

Top 5 Blushers

Vlogger Amelia Liana shares
her favourite blusher tricks

Cosmopolitan magazine's resident beauty vlogger
Amelia Liana presents her personal pick of blushers
in a friendly, conspiratorial style that's become
well-loved by her subscribers. From luxury brands
such as Tom Ford and Chanel, to more purse-friendly
options such as Milani, all of Amelia's choices are
well considered, as she takes pigmentation, formula
and colour into account. Whether you're looking
for a blusher to revitalize tired skin, a peachy
bronzing effect, a highlighting shimmer, an
illuminating tone, or a matte colour to balance
dramatic eye makeup, she's got it covered. Plus
each of her recommendations comes complete
with application tips and brush advice.

How to Cheat Supermodel Killer Cheekbones

Maximize your bone structure
with Charlotte Tilbury

We all lust after supermodel-style killer cheekbones and British makeup artist Charlotte Tilbury promises she can help you fake them. Charlotte says that from a young age, she noticed the effect a beautiful woman had entering a room and wanted to understand their secret weapon. And after a 20-year career working with some of the world's most attractive celebrities, including JLo, Penelope Cruz and Rihanna, she's learned all there is to know about maximizing your assets. This tutorial is a great beginner's guide to contouring cheeks, which will teach you how to sculpt cheekbones in just three simple steps, as well as how to avoid common mistakes.

http://youtu.be/h4ChiuRWPYI

How to Use Blusher

 Sali Hughes Beauty curates the ultimate blusher masterclass

The *Guardian*'s resident beauty columnist Sali Hughes is known for her straight-talking "beauty without the BS" style, so this is the video to watch if you want to know everything there is to know about blusher. And as it happens, there's a lot to learn as blusher is one of the least well used products around. Sali says she's constantly shocked at how many women leave the house with a full face of makeup but no blush – a look that she feels is incomplete and unbalanced. Sali shows how to get the "hotspot effect", reveals the best brushes for a natural application and explains what type of blusher is best suited to your skin type.

http://youtu.be/aRc_3iQiSoQ

NAIL IT

Perfect Polish Tutorials

Master a Professional-Looking Manicure

Lo Bosworth's easy
DIY mani

She may be one of the newer faces on the YouTube beauty scene, but Lo Bosworth – of *Laguna Beach* and *The Hills* fame – is quickly becoming one of the must-watch vloggers. "Want to skip the salon, save some dough, and paint your nails at home?" she asks, and then proceeds to show you exactly how to get professional results in half the time with her cool at-home manicure tutorial. Lo has insider tips on the best way to remove polish – she favours pure acetone – and how to trim cuticles for a neat finish. Plus, how to create the illusion of long slim nails with clever polish application, and make your varnish last much longer.

Newspaper Nail Art

Make headlines with Cutepolish's super-cool manicure

Cutepolish – created by vlogger Sandi Ball – has become the go-to channel for amazing, innovative nail designs that you can do at home and still wow your friends with. This step-by-step video shows how to create newspaper nails – yes, white nails with actual newspaper print over the top! After applying a white base coat and letting it dry, you dip fingers in rubbing alcohol and then hold a piece of newspaper over each nail for 15 seconds – which lifts the ink from the printed words onto your nails. You then apply a glossy top coat to prevent the ink coming off and add shine. A very urban, funky look that's so simple to achieve.

http://youtu.be/2kcdt4_5Ncc

DIY Homemade Matte Nail Polish

Rock grunge talons with Andrea
Brook's vampy varnish

Andrea Brooks of AndreasChoice is like the best
friend you wish you had – full of fabulous DIY beauty
tips and tricks. One of her favourite things is trying to
emulate the latest beauty looks without spending
any money, which means using makeup she already
has and kitchen cupboard essentials. Here she
demos how to mix simple cornstarch into your nail
polish before you apply it to create an amazing
on-trend matte effect. She then uses a clear gloss on
the top halves of the nails for a funky two-tone look.
She even shows any mistakes she make as she goes
along – and how to fix them.

Glamorous Neon Leopard Nail Art

Cutepolish's funky take
on feline fingernails

Why settle for one on-trend nail style when you can wear two at once! This eye-catching manicure may appear intricate, but with cutepolish, aka Sandi Ball's expert guidance, it is oh-so-easy to achieve. Sandi walks you through the design coat-by-coat, from the base to the final layer. All you need to recreate this neon take on a classic animal print look is a selection of white, black and brightly coloured nail varnishes, a makeup sponge and a toothpick. Sandi says she thinks of her nails as "tiny little canvases" and her creativity, aided by fun delivery, has helped her become the No. 1 nail art channel on YouTube. This video alone has been viewed more than a million times!

http://youtu.be/jaxKmvtYyMI

How to Do Gel Nails

Create everlasting polish at home
with Amelia Liana

Love gel nails but hate the hassle of going to the
beauty salon to have them applied – and then back
to the salon to have them removed? British beauty
blogger Amelia Liana has the answers. In this video
she shows how you can give yourself a gel manicure
at home, achieving a professional look with one of
the latest shop-bought kits. In just seven simple
steps Amelia guides you from using pre-application
cleanser and nail sanitizer to ensure your manicure
lasts, right through to a final application trick of
applying a little top coat over the tip to really seal in
the polish.

Water Spotted Nail Art

Master Cutepolish's original
nail technique

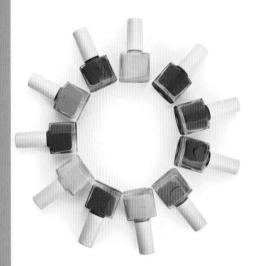

To get nails as intricately pretty as Cutepolish demos in this video you need professional nail art equipment, right? Well, no, actually: aside from polish in a variety of colours, all you need to create this look is a glass of warm water and hand sanitizer! We're not kidding! Who knew the humble handbag essential could be used on the nails as well as your mitts? Cutepolish's Sandi demonstrates how to create this dramatic look using her own "Water Spotted" technique. Don't miss her trick for making bright shades really pop with clever use of a white undercoat.

http://youtu.be/TnhfvuoBAMo

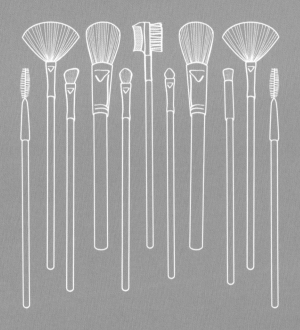

TOOLS OF THE TRADE

Brushes, Must-Have Products and More

Beginner's Makeup Starter Kit

RachhLoves lowdown on the basic beauty must-haves

If you're clueless when it comes to cosmetics, this great how-to from RachhLoves will help you start your makeup kit, listing all the basic cosmetics you can snag on a budget, and how best to use them. Rachel's essential selections include: a good foundation which should be applied onto the face with a brush (not forgetting to blend it into the neck to avoid lines), a light concealer for undereye circles and to use as an eyeshadow primer, and a simple blusher in pink. She then demos a neutral eye concept that works for everyday wear and pinky lip gloss to finish the easy, but perfectly polished look.

http://youtu.be/jaE3v4_4Co0

High-End Products I Won't Repurchase

Elle Fowler on how not
to waste money

One of YouTube's top beauty gurus, Elle certainly
knows her stuff when it comes to products. So this
vlog, which is dedicated to the designer products
she's forked out lots of money for that just didn't live
up to expectations, makes for fascinating viewing.
Watch her name and shame posh face powders from
Chanel, bland eyeshadows with poor texture and the
"plasticky" YSL lip stains everyone raved about, but
that she and her mum dislike intensely! Eyelash
primer also comes in for a drubbing, while Touche
Eclat is not a patch on L'Oreal's copycat version
– who knew?

http://youtu.be/bYi7LiGrxYQ

What's in My Travel Makeup Bag?

Louise Pentland's essential
beauty travel tips

Louise Pentland is a down-to-earth mum from the UK whose hit Sprinkleofglitter YouTube channel is guaranteed to make you laugh as she makes you over. This big personality is also brutally honest when it comes to product reviews – very useful for saving money. Here Louise takes us through her must-have products for trips away. Highlights include mini hairstyling products, dry shampoo, makeup compacts that include eyeshadow, blush and bronzer all together, all-in-one brow perfecting kits, cream eyeshadows for speedy application and sheer lipsticks to sweep on when you're on the move.

http://youtu.be/_kSOVmkhS38

How to Clean Makeup Brushes

TiffanyD reveals the quickest way
to refresh brushes

How often do you clean your makeup brushes? Be honest. All that lathering, rinsing and wringing is quite a dull chore. But it's important to look after your beauty tools, and doing so will certainly save you money, as with the proper care a good brush can last for years. Thankfully popular blogger TiffanyD has found the secret to speeding up brush cleaning, while also avoiding damage to sensitive hands. In this video she demonstrates how to clean as many as 20 brushes in just 5 minutes, with a special textured mitt. Not only that, she also shows the quickest way to dry brushes, which keeps the bristles flat and straight.

http://youtu.be/3_FHMQXQ_xl

How to Keep Your Teeth White

Discover the secret of Ilikeweylie's smile

Beauty vlogger Weylie's pearly white teeth have drawn plenty of admiring comments from the 1 million subscribers to her YouTube channel, so she's decided to let us in on the secret of her dazzling smile. And you'll be relieved to hear that her advice doesn't involve sitting in a dentist's chair! In fact, there's nothing scary or extreme at all – all that's required can be picked up from your local pharmacy (drugstore) and worked into your daily routine. In this video we find out why she uses two different types of toothpaste every time she brushes her teeth and the piece of teeth cleaning equipment she never leaves the house without – dental floss.

http://youtu.be/iWoVsvQoO0g

How to Pose for a Photograph

A Model Recommends' insider tips for the perfect pose

Model Ruth Crilly has more than a decade's worth of experience posing for fashion and beauty shoots and in this video she lets us in on the secrets professionals use to ensure they look their best in every pic. Top tips include never drop your chin – pull it up instead – don't always go side-on and smile fully for a natural look. Once you've mastered the art of being comfortable with your face and with the camera you'll soon find your most flattering camera pose – and the real trick, Ruth says, is to just repeat this signature pose every single time you're snapped!

http://youtu.be/FFx4befaGmQ

6 Fast Pharmacy Beauty Fixes

Emily Noel Eddington's speedy
solutions to common problems

Emily Noel Eddington spent years waking up at 1 a.m. to head off to her job as a morning TV news anchor, so she's certainly used to having to do her makeup in an hurry. In this beauty broadcast Emily uses just 6 products readily available from any pharmacy (drugstore) to demonstrate quick solutions to common makeup-related problems along with clever ways to get ready faster in the morning. Discover how to create a bun in seconds with one hairpin that does the work of 20 bobby pins. You'll also learn how to get an instant tanned look without damaging your skin and how to correct smudged liner with a nifty Revlon makeup eraser!

http://youtu.be/qYWYuQ3Msqk

Makeup Brush Masterclass

Pixiwoo's ultimate guide to every brush you'll ever need

Makeup brushes – there are so many to choose from and it can be confusing trying to remember which brush is best used for applying what. Thankfully Sam and Nic from Pixiwoo have created this thorough guide to makeup brushes, so never again will you be left pondering whether the brush in your bag is a "stippler" or a "buffer"! With tips on which brushes can be used for a multitude of purposes, as well as advice on how to clean your brushes to ensure they last for years, watching this video is essential before you buy another brush.

"Look Gorgeous Fast" Tricks

 GlamLifeGuru Tati shows off
her speedy techniques

In this "get-ready-with-me" style vlog, Tati from GlamLifeGuru showcases some of her tricks for making eyeliner and foundation look flawless, even when you're in a hurry. The target look is one that suits anyone regardless of eye shape or eye colour, and what's more, it's super-easy to master. If you feel the pop of blue liner is a little too bold for everyday, this look is easily toned down by swapping in a brown eyeliner. And don't miss Tati's advice on how to quickly create a soft cat-eye shape and her technique for ensuring the edge of your eyeshadow perfectly matches the wing of your eyeliner.

http://youtu.be/YT9z2f1vj44

Top 5 Makeup Mistakes

Learn from Emily Noel's slip-ups

Be it over-plucked brows, caked-on eyeshadow or badly blended contouring, we're all guilty of making the odd makeup mistake. Vlogger Emily's decided to open up about a few of her more cringe-worthy makeup mishaps, so that we can learn from her life lessons without ever having to experience the embarrassment for ourselves. The Illinois girl reveals the times when her gut instinct has led her astray as she "didn't have a tutorial to put on from YouTube to see what I was doing wrong". Luckily, you do, so take heed from Emily's mistakes – helpfully illustrated by cute old photos from her youth. Great tips include investing in a decent makeup brush set and avoiding harsh eyeliner.

http://youtu.be/Q1TmA5GzhYg

Summer Beauty Survival Kit

Look cool in the heat with Bubzbeauty's tips

This vlog's an absolute must-watch to prepare for scorching summer days. Bubzbeauty's Lindy Tsang reveals the contents of her summer survival kit which will apparently: "save your ass... well it's not going to literally save your ass, but it is going to be handy though!" she giggles. Learn how to take the shine out of oily skin, even on days when "it feels like you could fry chips on your face, it's so greasy," by using blotting sheets and powder foundation. Also useful are Lindy's tips on protecting your skin from the sun with a makeup primer containing SPF and tying your hair up and out of the way – using only one pin – for days when you're struggling in the heat.

http://youtu.be/03C5KsKrvdA

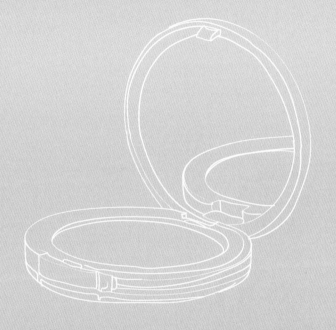

GET THE LOOK
Copy Your Favourite Famous Face

How to Look like a Bad Girl

Get homegirl cool with Michelle Phan's lookalike Rihanna

As YouTube's reigning beauty guru, Michelle Phan channels Rihanna for the ultimate "bad girl" look. Here she dispenses her usual insider know-how, explaining how to re-create sexy cat eyes with black liquid liner and strong berry lips for a vixen look and how to play it tough with contouring for razor cheekbones. In a step-by-step transformation, you see Phan accessorizing, Ri-Ri style, with heavy chains and metal gear, piercings (cheated) and stacked rings. The great thing about this video is that she shows techniques for so many key elements – brows, liner flick, cheekbones and dark lipstick. The Phan mantra she repeats here is worth remembering: "Hair frames the face; brows frame the eyes."

http://youtu.be/t6GnGaJh1hs

Snow White Makeup Tutorial

Become a Disney heroine
with Emma Pickles

"Mirror, mirror on the wall, who's the fairest of them all?" Ensure your mirror's answer is the one you want to hear with a little help from beauty vlogger Emma Pickles. Yorkshire lass Emma's motto is "We don't do natural here", and that's certainly true of the striking cartoon beauty she creates in this video! Watch spellbound as she talks and walks you through creating a flawless "Snow White" complexion, striking arched brows, innocent doe eyes, rosy cheeks and, of course, the signature red lips. If you enjoy this, check out her channel for a range of other Disney princess makeup tutorials, including Rapunzel and Ariel the Little Mermaid.

Adele's Grammys Red Carpet Look

Lauren Luke helps you channel
your inner diva

Vlogger Lauren Luke is on a mission to bring beauty to the masses. She says: "I believe strongly that beauty should be for everyone. I'm not a size zero model or even a trained makeup artist… Makeup should be something that you enjoy and not to be taken too seriously." In this video, the bold Brit recreates Adele's glam-Grammy look, complete with the singer's perfect porcelain skin tone, extra-long false eyelashes, retro-eyes, gold bronzer and matte red lips. Her zoomed-in close-ups at the end really help you visualize the look you're trying to achieve, while her honesty about which products work and which fail is priceless.

http://youtu.be/2cq1STBtHAE

Catching Fire: *Hunger Games*-Inspired Look!

Copy this red-hot Jennifer Lawrence look with Fleur DeForce

Brit vlogger Fleur DeForce has a wealth of insider tips, which means you can always trust this pretty presenter to get her hands on all the best new makeup and cool gadgets first. Here she recreates J-Law's "girl on fire" look from hit movie *The Hunger Games*, including flaming red, yellow and orange nails. Building up from a natural base, she adds smoky-outlined eyes and baby-pink lips. She then curls the lower sections of her hair using an amazing new curling tool and uses chalk – yes, chalk – to apply bright colours to the hair tips to give the impression of flames. Smokin'!

http://youtu.be/F0-4R2Th0fg

Hilary Duff's Blue Smoky Eye Look

Eman shares her take on funky celeb glamour

Eman, professional makeup artist and the creator of Mint Brushes, has years of experience working in the fashion and beauty industry and uses her insider knowledge to highlight the hottest makeup trends and to demonstrate simple ways to copy celebrity makeup looks. These bold, glittering blue eyes, inspired by singer and actress Hilary Duff, are not for the faint-hearted, but it is a great party look. Eman explains how to achieve the effect in clear and easy-to-follow steps, gradually building up blue colours – including navy and royal blue – until she's created a smoky, sexy, vibrant eye. Lips are kept largely neutral – pale pink and glossy – so they don't compete with the eyes for attention.

http://youtu.be/YJZrsNfPM_Q

How to Look like Daily Grace

Vloggers Grace Helbig and Tanya Burr team up for a natural look

Grace Helbig, aka "Daily Grace", is one of the vlogging world's comedic gems, which means her make up tutorials are as entertaining as they are useful. In this fun video, she teams up with British beauty guru Tanya Burr to demo how to get Grace's signature "no-makeup" look. It starts with foundation applied in a circular motion with a brush, before tidying her eyebrows with a shadow rather than pencil for a softer look. Next, light bronzer is used to contour her face and accentuate her cheekbones, followed by pinky purple blusher and highlighter. Peachy nude eyeshadow is then applied all over with a darker colour to add depth. Finally, gel eyeliner defines her eye and the look is completed with mid-pink lips. A simple but gorgeous look to try out.

http://youtu.be/4dfjLKnDLSU

Nicki Minaj: Super Bass Makeup

Destiny Godley's fierce
popstar look

LA-based vlogger Destiny Godley will teach you everything from how to establish a basic beauty routine to how to do your makeup like a celeb, which makes her channel a must-subscribe for beauty fiends and beginners alike. Here she shows how to channel Nicki Minaj's fierce and sexy Super Bass video look using bold white, purple and blue eyeshadows, lashings of black eyeliner and mascara and soft purple lips. She even recreates the music video with some of her own dance moves and lip-synching to get you in the mood. No wonder this fun vlog has enjoyed well over 2 million views!

http://youtu.be/eAWjfApFlpM

How to Look like Beyoncé

Transform yourself into a pop princess with Mystique

Beyoncé may be able to say "I woke up like this", but for those of us who need a little more help to look as flawless, vlogger Mystique has created this easy to follow guide to stealing her beauty style. They don't call Mystique the "Human Chameleon" for nothing – this beauty artist is famed for her ability to transform her face into the likeness of anyone from Marilyn Monroe to Johnny Depp! For Beyoncé she takes you step by step, starting with creating a base with primer then using contouring to create high cheekbones. Next she applies a series of shimmering eyeshadows, black eyeliner for a "cat eye" effect, silver glitter gel, false lashes, and nude glossy lips – all adding up to Beyoncé's unique superstar look.

Kim Kardashian-Inspired Smoky Eye Makeup

Perfect those smouldering peepers
with Eman

"Love her or hate her, you can't deny Kim Kardashian's makeup always looks amazing," points out Eman of successful YouTube channel MakeupByEman. Here she outlines in careful, close-up detail how to recreate those much-snapped sexy, sooty eyes in less than 12 minutes. In a reverse of the normal order of starting with lighter shades and building up to darker, Eman begins with a dark base on the top lid and then blends in a more coppery shade past the eye crease, before adding the lightest shade. Liquid liner is next, drawn carefully along the top lash line. Intense black shadow is then applied under the eye and on the top lash line. Finally, the whole eye is finished with lashings of black mascara and false eyelashes.

http://youtu.be/_kQhV4XzoGk

Lana Del Rey Makeup Tutorial

Tanya Burr's take on the singer's sexy retro look

Beauty blogging superstar Tanya Burr has a knack for recreating gorgeous celebrity makeup in a way you can easily follow. This tutorial takes you through singer Lana's look step by step, starting with a pale foundation for the perfect canvas and a matte eye base. Charcoal shadow is then used to darken the brows and add serious definition, before a series of increasingly darker matte brown shadows are blended onto the lids, and gel eyeliner applied for that winged retro shape on the upper lids. False lashes are vital for this look – including bottom lashes, which will be a first for many watchers but thankfully Tanya shows just how to apply them. No blush is used and for lips just a touch of pale, neutral lipstick.

http://youtu.be/_TQolVbF3kI

Lady Gaga "Poker Face" Tutorial

Get Gaga glamorous with Michelle Phan

Vlogger Michelle Phan is a women of a thousand faces and in this popular clip she helps you replicate Lady Gaga's sexy silver eye look as seen in her famous "Poker Face" music video. Michelle wants you to think of her as your "beauty bestie" and she speaks to all her audience as if they were old friends. Here she wisely advises that this isn't an everyday look and shouldn't be applied before work or school, but it is a real head-turner for clubbing or other "glamorous occasions". Michelle's feathering technique for softening harsh eyeliner, meanwhile, is simply an indispensible tip. Just remember: the wig is just for fun and the gold lightning bolt and leather gloves are optional!

http://youtu.be/YFMaLul1uxc

Angelina Jolie Makeup

Create Oscar-winning cat eyes
with Pixiwoo

Angelina Jolie is widely admired as one of the most beautiful women in the world. But British bloggers Pixiwoo want to let you in on a little secret – Mrs Pitt's look isn't all natural – Angelina applies just enough makeup to transform her face. Vlogging sisters Sam and Nic Chapman use this video to demystify the techniques that enhance Ange's naturally round eyes into her signature cat-eyed look. "Beauty isn't what you think it is," Nic explains, "someone like Angeline Jolie ... she wears her makeup a certain way because she's trying to create a certain shape with her eye." Here we learn a number of A-list tricks, from only using eyeliner on the outer half and corner for a feline shape to applying special false "corner" lashes.

http://youtu.be/pxox_MFpy7c

Lea Michele Smoky Eye Makeup

Red-carpet-ready eyes
with Eman

Glee star Lea Michele rocked this grey and black smoky eye look at the 2010 Grammys and it was voted one of the most popular award ceremony styles in a poll by professional makeup artist Eman. Little wonder Eman created this video to help her many subscribers learn how to recreate the look. But unlike some celeb makeup tutorials this one encourages experimenting to make the look your own, as "you have to do what works for you". Tips include using brown shades to warm up Lea's look, how to shape brows to open up your entire eye area and clever tricks for lining all around the eye area and cleaning up mistakes with concealer.

http://youtu.be/VD47yv2NfMw

How to Look like J-Lo

Mystique becomes the Latino
pop diva

"Beauty comes from inside," Jennifer Lopez once said, but that sentiment doesn't stop us admiring the Latin sensation's skin-deep sun-kissed style, and celeb copycat extraordinaire Mystique is here to show you just how to steal it. In this vlog she transforms herself into actress and singer J-Lo in just 6 minutes. Who knew it could be so easy? During the video we find out how to apply foundation that's similar to J-Lo's olive skin tone, how to get her golden glow by applying highlights in just the right places and finally how to fake her thick brows and contour-defined cheekbones so you too can look just like Jenny from the Block.

Victoria's Secret "Angel" Makeup

Catwalk perfection
with Tanya Burr

Lingerie giant Victoria's Secret is renowned for its catwalk shows featuring a cast of stunning supermodels such as Adriana Lima, Alessandra Ambrosio and Doutzen Kroes. Beauty blogger Tanya Burr is among the many admirers of the VS "angels" look, and here the enthusiastic Brit demonstrates how anyone can look as glowing, sexy and gorgeous as the catwalk queens. According to Tanya, Victoria's real secrets include applying glossy light shades on the lids to appear wide-eyed, faking a golden glow and shadow so subtle it looks like "just a huff of smoke around your eye". Make sure to watch this video all the way to the end for the bloopers!

http://youtu.be/IJMsU77qS5w

Game of Thrones: Daenerys Targaryen Look

Bring out your inner Khaleesi
with Michelle Phan

You'll be hard pushed to find a more dedicated *Game of Thrones* fan than YouTube superstar Michelle Phan and in this video she puts the makeup skills that have won her 6 million subscribers to work in transforming into her favourite character Daenerys Targaryen. Learn how you can achieve the Khaleesi's regal-yet-natural beauty, complete with sun-kissed skin, round open eyes and her bold full straight brows. Michele shares tips on how to use eyeshadow to create the illusion that your eyes are as deep set as actress Emilia Clarke's large green peepers, how to create full brows without them looking artificial, and how to reshape your lips to match Emilia's pretty pout with a natural rose glow.

http://youtu.be/tetymd_hoFA

Maleficent **Makeup Tutorial**

Kandee Johnson's magnificent masterclass

Movie villains often look more glamorous than the heroines, and the new queen of dark beauty has to be Angelina Jolie's Maleficent. For the live-action version of the famous Disney villain, Angelina's cheekbones are enhanced with prosthetics, but costume makeup chameleon Kandee Johnson's worked out how to recreate the look using just makeup. The American blogger transforms herself from cute to creepy with inside info from Ange's own makeup artists Rick Baker and Toni G. It's a dramatic look that's surprisingly easy to achieve with contouring. Angelina reportedly struck fear into the children on set, so perhaps this look is best saved for Halloween, rather than the school run!

http://youtu.be/ZPc33sD0U98

Katy Perry Makeup

Let out your inner California Girl
with Emma Pickles

All-American girl Katy Perry is known for her striking porcelain skin, bright lips and dramatic eye makeup. You too can be as "Unforgettable" with a little help from teen vlogger Emma Pickles. In just 2 minutes the Yorkshire lass shows how to fake Katy's chunky arched brows with a sharp eyebrow pencil and the tail of a pintail comb as a ruler, and how to use white liner first to make any colours on your eyes really pop. As Katy would say: "Baby, you're a firework! Come on, let your colours burst!" False lashes finish the eyes, while teen dream baby-pink is the required shade to recreate the pop star's pretty pout.

http://youtu.be/gQSvZ94N9SQ

The Author

Caroline Jones is a beauty, fashion and health journalist who has been a senior editor on several national newspapers and magazines in the UK. She is the author of five books, including *The Busy Girl's Guide to Looking Great* and *1001 Ways to Spend Less and Look Beautiful*. She lives in London with her daughter and husband.

Picture Credits

The publishers would like to thank the following sources for their kind permission to reproduce the pictures in this book.

All images are from Shutterstock except for the following:

Page 9 Lisa Maree Williams/Getty Images; 10 Cassandra Bankson; 11 Pavlinec/Thinkstock; 12 Pavlinec/Thinkstock; 13 Imagehub88/Thinkstock; 16 Fleur DeForce; 19 Cassandra Bankson; 20 Michael Bezjian/Getty Images; 22 Riccardo S. Savi/Getty Images; 23 Max Mumby/Indigo/Getty Images; 24 Mahbub Khan/Getty Images; 28 JB Lacroix/Getty Images; 30 Thomas Concordia/Getty Images; 31 Image Source/Getty Images; 32 Mike Marsland/Getty Images; 34 Patricia Bright; 36 Lauren Luke; 38 Rachel Murray/Getty Images; 39 Jessica Harlow; 41 Caiaimage/Getty Images; 42 Bryan Steffy/Billboard/Getty Images; 44 Jamie Grill/Getty Images; 46 Jamie McCarthy/Getty Images; 51 Joshua Blanchard/Getty Images; 55 Dave J Hogan/Getty Images; 56 Jessica Harlow; 57 Laura Cavanaugh/Getty Images; 62 Settaphan/Thinkstock; 66 Siobhán McDonnell, LetzMakeup; 67 Baibaz/Thinkstock; 69 Waring Abbott/Getty Images; 70 Fred Duvai/Getty Images; 74 Cassandra Bankson; 77 API/Getty Images; 79 Siobhán McDonnell, LetzMakeup; 80 Cassandra Bankson; 84 Patricia Bright; 86 David Livingston/Getty Images; 89 Cultura RM/Franck Sauvaire/Getty Images; 91 Tetra Images/Getty Images; 100 The Image Bank/Getty Images; 103 Dave J Hogan/Getty Images; 104 Stone/Getty Images; 110 Michelle Phan; 111 Emma Pickles; 112 Dan MacMedan/Getty Images; 113 Dave M. Benett/Getty Images; 115 Paul Redmond/Getty Images; 116 Jason Merritt/Getty Images; 117 Ian Gavan/Getty Images; 118 Jeffrey Mayer/Getty Images; 119 Neil Mockford/Getty Images; 120 Jo Hale/Getty Images; 121 Ethan Miller/Getty Images; 122 Gregg DeGuire/Getty Images; 123 Gregg DeGuire/Getty Images; 125 Michelle Phan; 126 © Moviestore collection Ltd/Alamy; 127 Emma Pickles.

Every effort has been made to acknowledge correctly and contact the source and/or copyright holder of each picture and Carlton Books Limited apologises for any unintentional errors or omissions, which will be, corrected in future editions of this book.